My First Year

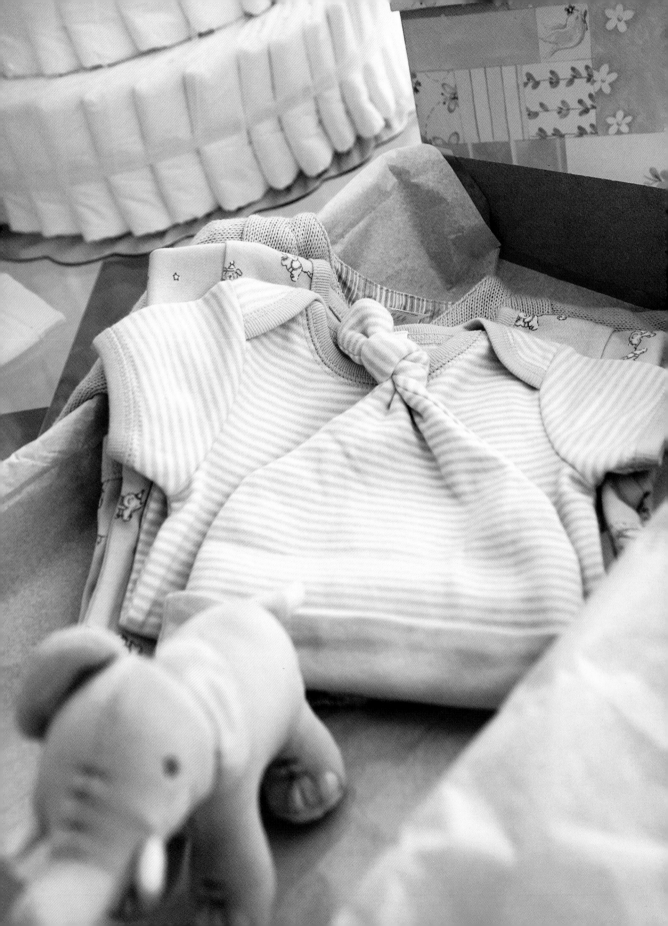

My First Year

my photo here

YOUR BABY'S ONE-YEAR RECORD

Vermilion

The birth of every new baby
is a magical event and the early days
of your child's life are wonderful to
look back on. But these first precious
days, weeks and months race by in a
flash, and it's all too easy to forget all
the little details. To keep memories
fresh, create your child's own record
in this delightful book – it'll become
a lasting keepsake to treasure
in the years to come.

Before I was born

* *

My mum is called

....

My dad is called

....

My sister(s) is/are called

....

....

My brother(s) is/are called

....

....

The following people came to my baby shower

....

....

....

They gave us these presents

....

....

....

....

....

* * * * * * * * * * * * * * * * *

Before I was born

My parents' special name for me before I was born
....

My mum first felt me move on
....

Some memories from the time before I was born
....

....

....

What my parents were doing just before I was born
....

....

My family tree

My great-grandparents

....

....

....

....

My grandparents

....

....

My aunts and uncles

....

....

....

....

My cousins

....

....

....

....

My family tree

My mum   My dad

. . . .

My brothers and sisters

. . . .

. . . .

Me

. . . .

Some special memories of my family

. . . .

. . . .

. . . .

. . . .

. . . .

. . . .

. . . .

. . . .

My birth

★ ★

My due date was

....

I was born on

....

The day of the week was

....

The time of day/night was

....

The place was

....

The people present were

....

....

My midwife was called

....

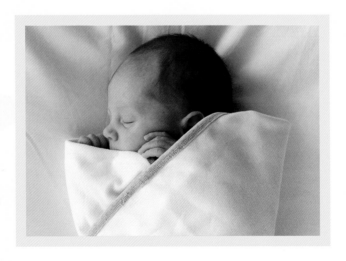

★ ★

My birth

★ ★

my photo here

I weighed in at

....

I measured

....

My eyes were

....

My hair was

....

Some major world events on my day of birth were

....

My parents' memories of my birth were

....

....

★ ★

My first pictures...

my photo here

my photo here

My first pictures...

my photo here

my photo here

Coming home – my early days

I wake up at

....

I have my feeds at

....

I have my naps at

....

I go to bed at

....

My nursery has these things in it

....

....

....

....

....

....

....

....

....

....

My visitors

★ ★

When I came home from hospital these people came to see me

....

....

....

Some of the things they said to me were

....

....

....

....

★ ★

My visitors

★ ★

photo of me and my visitors

★ ★

Gifts and cards

✳ ✳ ✳ ✳ ✳ ✳ ✳ ✳ ✳ ✳ ✳ ✳ ✳ ✳ ✳ ✳ ✳

My friends and family have been very generous.

Here are the gifts and cards I received

✳ ✳ ✳ ✳ ✳ ✳ ✳ ✳ ✳ ✳ ✳ ✳ ✳ ✳ ✳ ✳ ✳

My hand prints

Here are outlines of my hands when I was   months old

My foot prints

Here are outlines of my feet when I was _____ months old

Sleeps

I first slept in a cot on

....

I slept through the night for the first time on

....

My 'bedtime' is at

....

My favourite lullaby is

....

and the person who sings it best is

....

My favourite cuddly toy is

....

My favourite bedtime book is

....

My special bedtime ritual is

....

....

....

Here are some bedtime memories

....

....

....

....

Feeds

I was breastfed until

....

I was bottlefed until

....

My first taste of real food was on

....

I held a spoon for the first time on

....

I tried finger food for the first time on

....

I fed myself for the first time on

....

I drank from a beaker for the first time on

....

I sat in a highchair for the first time on

....

My favourite foods are

....

....

My least-favourite foods are

....

....

Here are some mealtime memories

....

....

My bathtimes

✳ ✳

I went in the baby bath for the first time on

. . . .

I went in the big bath for the first time on

. . . .

My favourite bath toys are

. . . .

. . . .

My favourite bath games are

. . . .

. . . .

Here are some bathtime memories

. . . .

. . . .

. . . .

. . . .

. . . .

. . . .

. . . .

✳ ✳

My naming ceremony

My name is

....

It means

....

Some famous people who share my name

....

....

....

My parents chose my name because

....

....

My naming ceremony

My godparents are

. . . .

. . . .

The following people came to my naming ceremony

. . . .

. . . .

. . . .

. . . .

. . . .

I wore this outfit for my naming ceremony

. . . .

My naming ceremony was held at

. . . .

The ceremony was performed by

. . . .

I was given these presents/cards

. . . .

. . . .

. . . .

Photos of my naming ceremony

photo of me and my visitors

photo of me and my visitors

Photos of my naming ceremony

photo of me and my visitors

photo of me and my visitors

My favourite things

I first noticed my mobile on

....

I first started playing with my baby gym on

....

I first held my teddy on

....

I first went in a baby bouncer on

....

My special cuddly toy is a

....

My favourite rattle is

....

My favourite toy is

....

My favourite things

Here are some things that make me laugh

....

....

....

....

....

....

....

....

My firsts

★ ★

I first lifted my head on
....

I first followed a moving object with my eyes on
....

I first played with my hands on
....

I first held a rattle on
....

I first rolled over on
....

I first discovered my feet on
....

I first sat up all by myself on
....

I first crawled on
....

I first pulled myself up to stand on
....

I first climbed up the stairs on
....

I first climbed down the stairs on
....

I took my first steps on
....

I first started walking around the furniture on
....

★ ★

My firsts

◆ ◆

I first moved my eyes to watch you on

....

I first started babbling on

....

I smiled for the first time on

....

I laughed for the first time on

....

I copied noises for the first time on

....

I started 'shouting' on

....

I started 'singing' on

....

My first 'words' were

....

I first pointed on

....

I first waved goodbye on

....

I first clapped my hands on

....

I first grasped something with my finger and thumb on

....

I first played 'peek-a-boo' on

....

◆ ◆

My firsts

I wore my first pair of shoes on

I had my first haircut on

My first tooth came through on

My second tooth came through on

My third tooth came through on

Here is a lock of my hair

My first activities and outings

I first went swimming on

....

I first went on a swing on

....

I went to my first party on

....

I first 'helped' with gardening on

....

I first 'helped' with cooking on

....

I first went to the park on

....

I first went to my grandparents' home on

....

I first went in a buggy on

....

I first went in a car on

....

I first went on a train on

....

I first went on a bus on

....

I first went on a plane on

....

....

My first activities and outings

Here are some memories of my early activities and outings

....

....

....

....

....

Photos of my activities and outings

photo of my activity/outing here

photo of my activity/outing here

Photos of my activities and outings

photo of my activity/outing here

photo of my activity/outing here

My first playdates and parties

I went to play with

....

on

....

I went to a party on

....

My best friends are

....

Here are some memories of my early social life

....

....

....

Photos of my activities and outings

photo of my activity/outing here

photo of my activity/outing here

My first playdates and parties

I went to play with

....

on

....

I went to a party on

....

My best friends are

....

Here are some memories of my early social life

....

....

....

My first holiday

The first time I went on holiday was

We went on holiday to

These are the people who came with us

These are some people we met

We stayed in

My favourite activities were

Here are some memories of my first holiday

Photos of my first holiday

my holiday photo here

my holiday photo here

Photos of my first holiday

my holiday photo here

my holiday photo here

My first Christmas

❋ ❋

Father Christmas came down the chimney and brought me the following

. . . .

. . . .

. . . .

My parents gave me

. . . .

. . . .

. . . .

My friends and family gave me

. . . .

. . . .

. . . .

These are some people who were there too

. . . .

. . . .

. . . .

I wore

. . . .

I ate the following for Christmas dinner

. . . .

. . . .

. . . .

❋ ❋

Photos of my first christmas

❄ ❄

Here are some special memories of my first Christmas

. . . .

. . . .

. . . .

. . . .

. . . .

. . . .

. . . .

. . . .

my Christmas photo here

❄ ❄

Photos of my first christmas

my Christmas photo here

my Christmas photo here

Playtimes

☐	I love to bang on my toy drum	☐	I like to splash with water
☐	I like to play with bubbles	☐	I love to crunch wrapping paper
☐	I like toys on wheels	☐	I like to play with bricks
☐	I like rolling balls	☐	I love to chew things

Playtimes

Here is one of my first artistic efforts…

Medical check-ups

✖ ✖

My immunisations

....

My eyesight tests

....

My hearing tests

....

My illnesses

....

My allergies

....

My blood group

....

My doctor

....

My dentist

....

Special things that might be useful to know about when I grow up

....

....

....

....

....

✖ ✖

My first birthday

★ ★

This is who came to my first birthday party

. . . .

. . . .

. . . .

. . . .

. . . .

My cake was in the shape of a

. . . .

I wore this outfit

. . . .

I received these brilliant presents

. . . .

. . . .

. . . .

. . . .

. . . .

Here are some memories of my first birthday

. . . .

. . . .

. . . .

. . . .

. . . .

★ ★

Photos of my first birthday

★ ★

my birthday photo here

my birthday photo here

★ ★

Photos of my first birthday

★ ★

my birthday photo here

my birthday photo here

★ ★

How much am I growing?

* *

MY HEIGHT

My length at birth
. . . .

3 months
. . . .

6 months
. . . .

9 months
. . . .

1 year
. . . .

MY WEIGHT

My birth weight
. . . .

3 months
. . . .

6 months
. . . .

9 months
. . . .

1 year
. . . .

* *

1 3 5 7 9 10 8 6 4 2

Published in 2011 by Vermilion, an imprint of Ebury Publishing

Ebury Publishing is a Random House Group company

The Random House Group Limited Reg. No. 954009

Addresses for companies within the Random House Group can be found at
www.randomhouse.co.uk

A CIP catalogue record for this book is available from the British Library

The Random House Group Limited supports The Forest Stewardship
Council (FSC), the leading international forest certification organisation. All our
titles that are printed on Greenpeace approved FSC certified paper carry the FSC logo.
Our paper procurement policy can be found at
www.randomhouse.co.uk/environment

Designed by Isobel Gillan
Written by Jo Godfrey Wood, Bookworx

Printed and bound in China by C & C Offset Printing Co., Ltd

ISBN: 9780091939861

Copies are available at special rates for bulk orders.
Contact the sales development team on 020 7840 8487 for more information.

To buy books by your favourite authors and register for offers, visit www.randomhouse.co.uk

PICTURE CREDITS

front cover © Fernando Bengoechea/Beateworks/Corbis; p.1 © Kiselev Andrey Valerevich/
Shutterstock; p.2 © Ocean/Corbis; p.5 © Niki Mareschal/Getty; p.6 © Datacraft Co Ltd/
Photolibrary; p.7 © France Ruffenach/Getty; p.10 © Tom Grill/Getty; p.14 © Tom Merton/Getty;
p.15 © Amanda Lynn/First Light/Corbis; p.16 © Marcy Maloy/Getty; p.17 © Dorling Kindersley/
Getty; p.18 © Robert Daly/Getty; p.19 © Image Source/Getty; p.22 © Peter Reali/Corbis; p.25
© Achim Sass/Photolibrary; pp.26–27 © Steven Errico/Getty; p.28 © Image Source/Corbis; p.29
© Lauren Nicole/Getty; p.32 © Frederic Cirou/PhotoAlto/Corbis; p.33 © Tom Merton/Getty; p.35 ©
Absodels/Getty; p.36 © Julia Smith/Getty; p.39 © TongRo Image Stock/Corbis; p.41 © artparadigm/
Getty; p.44 © Virgo Productions/Corbis; p.45 © Jamie Grill/Photolibrary; p.46 © MIXA Co. Ltd./
Photolibrary; p.50 © Datacraft/Getty; p.51 © Lew Robertson/Corbis; p.54 © Image Source/Getty;
p.57 © Annie Engel/Corbis; p.58 © Jamie Grill/Tetra Images/Corbis; p.59 © Monalyn Gracia/Corbis;
p.62 © Jade Brookbank/Getty